Gooden, Rima.

Gooden, Gregory.

Chloe Learns: Clever Chloe's Lemonade Adventure / Rima & Gregory Gooden.

First Edition, December 2023

ISBN: 9798872411895

CLEVER CHLOE'S LEMONADE ADVENTURE

RIMA GOODEN

GREG GOODEN

CHLOE LEARNS
SERIES

GOODEN
PUBLISHING HOUSE

Clever Chloe's Lemonade Stand

THIS CHLOE LEARNS BOOK BELONGS TO:

_____

_____

_____

_____

Table of Contents

The Idea

Clever Chloe's mind buzzed with excitement as she walked past a bustling lemonade stand on her way home from school. The delicious aroma of fresh lemons filled the air, sparking an idea in Chloe's mind. "I want to have my own lemonade stand too!" she exclaimed, a wide smile spreading across her face.

Chloe hurried home and burst through the door, eager to share her newfound ambition with her parents. They were sitting at the kitchen table, sipping their evening tea. "Mom, Dad, guess what?" Chloe beamed. Her parents looked up, curious about their daughter's excitement.

"I want to start my own lemonade stand!" Chloe exclaimed, bouncing on her toes.

Her mom raised an eyebrow, intrigued. "That sounds like a wonderful idea! Starting a business can be a great learning experience. How do you plan to make it happen?"

Chloe's mind raced with ideas. She replied, "I'll need a stand, lemons, sugar, cups, and a catchy name for my lemonade stand!"
Her dad smiled and nodded. "That's a good start. This will teach you about earning money and running a small business."

Chloe's eyes sparkled with determination. "I'm ready to learn, Dad. I'll be the cleverest lemonade stand owner ever!"

Together, Chloe and her parents sat down at the kitchen table, brainstorming ideas for her lemonade stand. They discussed the importance of finding a prime location, making enticing signage, and selecting a catchy name.

"How about 'Clever Chloe's Lemonade Stand'?" her mom suggested. "It reflects your cleverness and enthusiasm!"

Chloe clapped her hands in excitement. "I love it! Clever Chloe's Lemonade Stand it is!"

They made a list of the supplies they would need: lemons, sugar, cups, a pitcher, and a table. Chloe's dad explained that they would also need to keep track of their expenses and earnings.

"Running a business means understanding your costs," he said. "This way, you'll know how much to charge for your lemonade." As Chloe prepared for bed that night, she couldn't contain her excitement. She imagined the colorful sign she would create and the refreshing lemonade she would serve to her customers. She knew it would take hard work, but she was eager to embark on her entrepreneurial journey.

With dreams of lemonade stands dancing in her head, Chloe drifted off to sleep, eagerly anticipating the start of her new adventure.

Preparations

The morning sun peeked through Chloe's bedroom window, casting a warm glow on her face. It was the day she had been eagerly anticipating—the day to prepare for Clever Chloe's Lemonade Stand. Chloe stretched her arms and yawned, feeling a mix of excitement and nervousness.

Today was the day she would start turning her lemonade dreams into reality, but she knew careful preparations were necessary to ensure everything ran smoothly. She quickly got out of bed and made her way downstairs, where her parents were waiting for her, ready to assist with the preparations.

"Good morning, Clever Chloe! Are you ready to get everything ready for your lemonade stand?" her mom asked, a gleam of anticipation in her eyes.

Chloe nodded eagerly. "Yes, Mom! I can't wait!"

They gathered around the kitchen table, and Chloe brought out the list of supplies she had made the previous day. Together, they reviewed it, making sure nothing was missing.

"First, we need to gather all the ingredients for your delicious lemonade," her dad suggested, smiling.

Chloe retrieved the list and checked off the items as they discussed them one by one. Fresh lemons, sugar, cups, and napkins were essential. Her mom suggested adding colorful straws for a festive touch, but they decided to keep other creative ideas, like flavored variations, for future brainstorming sessions.

"Now we just need to figure out the perfect spot for the stand," her dad said thoughtfully. "It's important to choose a location where people will stop and enjoy a refreshing drink."

Chloe pondered for a moment, then exclaimed, "How about the local park? It's always busy on sunny days, and lots of families go there to play and relax."

Her parents nodded in agreement, impressed by her thoughtful suggestion. They began discussing the logistics of setting up near the park and how they could make the stand visible and appealing to potential customers.

While her parents gathered the necessary supplies, Chloe took a moment to reflect on the financial aspect of her lemonade stand.

She remembered their conversation about covering costs and making a profit. Determined to understand the business side, she took out her notepad and carefully calculated the estimated expenses. Chloe's brows furrowed in concentration. "I want my lemonade to be affordable for everyone. How about 50 cents per cup?" Her parents smiled, impressed by her thoughtful approach.

"That's a great start, Chloe. Let's write down everything you'll need and revisit the price once we finalize your recipe and setup" her mom said.

As the preparations wrapped up, Chloe's excitement grew. She could picture the colorful stand, the smiling customers, and the refreshing lemonade that would brighten their day. With everything ready, she knew she was one step closer to achieving her dream.

Creating a Product

The sun peeked through Chloe's bedroom window, signaling the start of a new day filled with possibilities. As she opened her eyes, her mind brimmed with excitement about the next phase of Clever Chloe's Lemonade Stand—creating the perfect product.

Chloe hopped out of bed, slipping into her lemon-themed outfit—a bright yellow shirt adorned with lemons and matching shorts. She hurried downstairs, eager to join her parents in the kitchen.

"Good morning, Clever Chloe! Ready to create the most delicious lemonade?" her dad greeted her with a smile.

Chloe nodded with enthusiasm. "Absolutely, Dad! I want my lemonade to be irresistible!" Her parents chuckled at her determination as they gathered in the kitchen.

Chloe's mom took out a cutting board, while her dad prepared a large bowl of fresh lemons and a juicer.

Chloe eagerly grabbed a lemon, feeling its vibrant yellow skin beneath her fingertips. She took a deep breath, savoring the aroma.

"First, let's juice the lemons," Chloe explained, placing a lemon on the juicer and squeezing it to extract its fresh juice.

As they worked together, Chloe's mom emphasized the importance of quality control. "Chloe, we want every glass of lemonade to taste perfect. We need to make sure there are no seeds or pulp in the juice."

Chloe nodded and carefully strained the freshly squeezed juice through a sieve, ensuring a smooth and refreshing result.

"Now comes the fun part—sweetening the lemonade!" Chloe exclaimed, her eyes gleaming with anticipation.

Her dad handed her the pitcher. Chloe took a moment to assess the amount and decided, "We'll need to add some sugar for the perfect balance of sweetness."

She poured sugar into a measuring cup and added it to the pitcher.

Chloe's mom suggested they taste the lemonade to ensure the flavors were balanced. "Clever Chloe, let's take a sip and see if it needs any adjustments."

Chloe took a thoughtful sip, her taste buds dancing with delight. She considered the sweetness and tanginess and, with a smile, declared, "It's delicious, but I think a touch more sweetness will make it better."

Together, they added a little more sugar, fine-tuning the recipe until they achieved the perfect flavor. Chloe beamed, proud of her ability to adjust and refine the recipe.

Once the final batch was ready, they carried their lemonade and cups outside to the backyard. The sun was shining, and it felt like the perfect spot to enjoy their creation together.

As they enjoyed the lemonade, Chloe had an idea. "What if we made a special version with a twist? Like mint-infused lemonade!"

Her mom raised an eyebrow with interest. "That is very creative!"

Chloe giggled. "We could call it our secret recipe!"

Her dad nodded. "I like it! Let's see what we can come up with."

Her parents exchanged amused glances. "We do have mint in the garden," her mom said with a smile. "That could be a fun addition."

Chloe's eyes lit up. "Let's try it!"

Her dad stood up, stretching. "Alright, mint mission—let's go!"

They finished their lemonade and headed off together to gather the fresh ingredient.

They plucked fresh mint leaves from their garden and added a few to the lemonade.

After letting the flavors mix, they tasted the new creation.

"This is amazing!" Chloe exclaimed. "It's refreshing and unique. We have to offer this at the stand!"

Her parents agreed, impressed by her creativity. Inspired by their success, they spent the afternoon perfecting the mint-infused lemonade recipe, making careful notes so they could recreate it later.

Chloe's mom added one final reminder: "Be sure to write down your recipe, Clever Chloe, so you'll always have it for the future!"

As evening approached, Chloe felt a sense of pride in the product they had created together. With the recipe finalized, her mind filled with anticipation for the next chapter of her entrepreneurial journey. As she closed her eyes that night, she imagined the smiling faces of customers enjoying her refreshing lemonade.

Pricing Strategies

Clever Chloe woke up with a spark of excitement, knowing that today she would delve into the world of pricing strategies for her lemonade stand. As she got ready for the day, she couldn't help but wonder how much she should charge for her refreshing mint-infused lemonade.

Downstairs, Chloe joined her parents at the kitchen table. They greeted her with warm smiles, ready to guide her through the intricacies of pricing her product.

"Clever Chloe, setting the right price is crucial for your lemonade stand," her dad began. "It needs to cover your costs while still being attractive to your customers."

Chloe nodded, understanding the importance of finding a balance. "What about 50 cents per cup?" she asked, thinking it sounded affordable and appealing.

Her dad smiled but paused thoughtfully. "That's a good starting point, Chloe, but let's make sure it's enough to cover everything. We'll need to take a closer look at the numbers."

"We need to make sure that the price you set covers all the expenses while providing a reasonable value for your customers. Don't forget to consider your effort, too—your time is valuable."

They gathered the list of expenses required to make the lemonade: lemons, sugar, cups, napkins, and other supplies.

Chloe's dad guided her through the calculations, helping her estimate the cost per cup. As they worked through the details, Chloe began to understand that pricing wasn't just about covering costs—it was about reflecting the quality of her product and the effort she put into making it. Chloe's brows furrowed in thought. "What about 75 cents per cup? It's still affordable but gives us some profit too."

Her parents nodded in agreement. "That sounds reasonable, Clever Chloe," her dad said. "But what if we also offer a bundle deal? It could encourage customers to buy more and increase your sales."

Chloe's eyes lit up with excitement. "That's a great idea, Dad! How about we offer 2 cups for $1.40?"

Her mom smiled. "By offering a bundle deal, customers will see the value and be more inclined to buy multiple cups. It's a win-win situation!"

With the pricing finalized, they packed their supplies, including the pitcher of mint-infused lemonade, cups, and materials to create a colorful sign displaying the prices.

Arriving at the park, Chloe and her parents began setting up the lemonade stand. Chloe took the time to create an eye-catching sign that caught the attention of passersby. She carefully arranged the words and colors, ensuring it reflected the quality and creativity of her lemonade.

As they stepped back to admire their setup, Chloe's excitement grew. She knew that the value she offered was reflected in every cup of her refreshing lemonade.

With the pricing strategy in place and the stand ready for business, Chloe eagerly awaited the arrival of the first customers. She stood confidently behind the counter, her sign clearly showing the prices and special offers.

As people walked by, she greeted them with a friendly smile and invited them to try her lemonade. Curious customers began to gather. Chloe explained the different pricing options, including her special bundle deal.

Families and groups were drawn to the "2 cups for $1.40" offer, while individual customers appreciated the affordability of a single cup.

By the end of the day, Chloe and her parents counted their earnings and reflected on the success of their pricing strategies. Chloe had not only covered her costs but also made a healthy profit.

"I'm so proud of you, Clever Chloe," her mom said, a glimmer of admiration in her eyes. "You've learned the art of pricing and provided excellent value to your customers."

Chloe beamed with satisfaction, realizing the importance of pricing in running a business.

As the lemonade stand closed for the day, Chloe felt a renewed sense of confidence. She couldn't wait to explore new opportunities and continue her entrepreneurial journey.

Spreading
the Word

The sun rose high in the sky, casting a warm glow over Clever Chloe's Lemonade Stand. Today, Chloe was ready to take the next big step in her entrepreneurial journey—spreading the word about her delicious mint-infused lemonade.

Chloe hurried downstairs, her mind buzzing with ideas. She found her parents at the kitchen table, sipping their morning coffee. "Good morning, Clever Chloe!" her dad greeted her. "Are you ready to discover the power of marketing?"

Chloe nodded eagerly. "Yes, Dad! I want everyone to know about Clever Chloe's Mint-Infused Lemonade!"

Her parents exchanged knowing smiles. They understood the importance of effective marketing in reaching a wider audience. Together, they brainstormed ways to spread the word about Chloe's lemonade stand.

First on their list was creating eye-catching flyers. Chloe drew colorful lemons and mint leaves on pieces of paper, while her parents helped her write the details of her lemonade stand—its location, hours of operation, and the prices.

With a pile of vibrant flyers in hand, Chloe and her parents headed to the local community center. They pinned the flyers on bulletin boards and handed them out to passersby, sharing their excitement about the stand.

Next, they turned to social media. Chloe's parents helped her take enticing photos of the lemonade stand setup, capturing the vibrant colors and refreshing appeal of the lemonade. They created a dedicated social media page for Clever Chloe's Lemonade Stand and shared the photos along with captivating captions.

Chloe's mom explained the importance of engaging with the online community. "Clever Chloe, it's essential to respond to comments, answer questions, and build connections with your potential customers. Show them how much care you put into your lemonade stand."

Under her parents' supervision, Chloe diligently responded to comments and thanked people for their support.

Her parents also ensured she followed best practices for internet security and privacy, creating a safe and positive online experience.

The engagement grew steadily, attracting more followers and generating genuine excitement for Clever Chloe's Lemonade Stand. Encouraged by the success of their efforts, Chloe and her parents decided to reach out to the local newspaper to share her story.

To their delight, the newspaper loved the idea. A friendly journalist visited Chloe's lemonade stand, conducted an interview, and took photos of her serving her lemonade.

When the article was published, it featured Clever Chloe's Lemonade Stand on the front page of the local section.

The story introduced Chloe's journey to the entire community, drawing even more attention to her business.

As days went by, Chloe saw the impact of her marketing efforts. People flocked to her lemonade stand, excited to try the refreshing mint-infused lemonade they had heard so much about.

Chloe's smile widened as she served her growing customer base. She knew that her hard work, creativity, and determination had paid off. The thrill of entrepreneurship coursed through her veins, inspiring her to continue exploring new marketing ideas.

As the sun set on another successful day at the lemonade stand, Chloe and her parents reflected on the power of spreading the word.

"Chloe, you've learned the art of marketing," her dad praised. "You've shown how important it is to create a buzz around your product and connect with your community."

Chloe's mom added, "Your passion and dedication have shone through in every flyer, social media post, and interaction with customers. It's clear why everyone loves Clever Chloe's Mint-Infused Lemonade." With her lemonade stand thriving, Chloe felt a renewed sense of confidence.

Customer Service

The sun peeked over the horizon, casting a warm glow on Clever Chloe's Lemonade Stand. Today, Chloe's entrepreneurial journey would lead her to explore the crucial aspect of customer service. She knew that providing an exceptional experience would keep her customers coming back for more.

Chloe started her day with a sense of purpose. She joined her parents in the kitchen, ready for the day's adventure.

"Chloe, great customer service can make all the difference," her mom explained. "It's about making your customers feel valued and creating a positive experience." Chloe understood that the quality of her product was just one part of the equation— the way she treated her customers would set her apart

Her dad added, "Remember, Clever Chloe, a smile and friendly attitude can go a long way. Take the time to listen to your customers, address their needs, and make their visit to your lemonade stand memorable."

With those words in mind, Chloe eagerly set up her lemonade stand for the day.

She arranged the cups, the pitcher of mint-infused lemonade, and the sign displaying the prices. Chloe greeted each customer with a genuine smile, asking how their day was going and listening carefully to their preferences. Whether they wanted individual cups or the "2 cups for $1.40" deal, Chloe made sure their experience was personalized.

She took extra care in serving her customers, ensuring each cup was filled to the brim with refreshing lemonade. Chloe's passion for her product shone through as she shared the story behind her creation, describing the fresh ingredients and her dedication to providing a unique experience. Chloe's parents watched with pride as she interacted with each customer.

A group of children approached the lemonade stand, their eyes wide with excitement. Chloe's heart swelled with joy as she realized she had become a local favorite among the younger crowd.

"Hi there!" Chloe greeted them enthusiastically. "Are you ready for some delicious mint-infused lemonade?"

The children nodded eagerly, their excitement contagious. Chloe took the time to chat with them, sharing fun facts about lemons and mint while answering their curious questions. She created a welcoming atmosphere where they felt comfortable and valued.

Chloe offered samples to those who were unsure, patiently answered questions, and graciously thanked everyone for their support.

Inspired by the power of customer service and eager to enhance the overall experience for her customers, Chloe came up with a brilliant idea. She decided to create a special backdrop sign specifically for people to take social media pictures at her lemonade stand.

Chloe spent hours working on the design, carefully selecting vibrant colors and incorporating elements that represented the essence of Clever Chloe's Mint-Infused Lemonade. She painted large lemons and mint leaves on the sign and added catchy phrases like "Sip and Smile." She also made sure to include the hashtag #CleverChloesLemonadeStand.

The next day, as Chloe set up her lemonade stand, she proudly displayed the new backdrop sign in a prominent spot. She positioned it in such a way that customers could take photos with it while enjoying their refreshing lemonade. She hoped that these social media pictures would not only create a memorable experience for her customers but also serve as free marketing for her lemonade stand.

To her delight, the idea was an instant hit. Customers flocked to the sign, eagerly posing for pictures and sharing them on their social media accounts. The colorful backdrop and the mention of Clever Chloe's Mint-Infused Lemonade spread across various platforms, reaching a wider audience beyond her local community.

Chloe's smile grew wider as she witnessed the power of her idea. The social media posts quickly generated buzz, with comments and shares from people who hadn't yet visited. It was a win-win situation —an opportunity for customers to capture and share their enjoyable moments at the lemonade stand while promoting Clever Chloe's Mint-Infused Lemonade to their friends and followers.

As Chloe wrapped up another successful day at the lemonade stand, she couldn't help but feel a sense of accomplishment. The combination of exceptional customer service and the backdrop sign had created a memorable experience for her customers. She knew that word-of-mouth and social media were powerful tools that could propel her lemonade stand to new heights.

As Chloe started to close her lemonade stand for the day, she exchanged happy glances with her parents. "Clever Chloe, your dedication to providing an exceptional experience has paid off," her dad praised. "Not only have you created a memorable customer experience, but you've also tapped into the power of free marketing through social media."

Chloe felt a sense of pride and excitement. She knew that she had discovered a valuable lesson—the importance of creating a memorable customer experience and utilizing social media as a marketing tool. With each chapter of her entrepreneurial journey, Chloe continued to learn, grow, and uncover new opportunities to take Clever Chloe's Lemonade to greater heights.

Giving Back

Clever Chloe woke up with a renewed sense of purpose. Today, she would focus on giving back. Success, she realized, wasn't just about financial gain but about creating a positive impact on others.

At the breakfast table, she shared her thoughts with her parents.

"Giving back to the community is a wonderful way to show gratitude for their support," her mom said. "It's an opportunity to make a meaningful difference and build stronger connections." Her dad nodded. "There are so many ways to give back—donating a portion of your earnings, organizing fundraisers, or getting involved in community events."

Inspired, Chloe proposed, "What if we donate part of the lemonade stand profits to a children's charity? That way, we can help other kids who need it."

Her parents exchanged proud smiles. "That's a fantastic idea," her mom said. "Let's find a charity that aligns with our values."

After some research, they chose an organization supporting underprivileged children by providing educational resources, school supplies, and mentoring programs. Chloe felt a deep connection to the cause and was eager to contribute.

Together, they prepared for a special fundraising day at the lemonade stand. Chloe designed bright, colorful posters explaining their mission and the charity they were supporting. Flyers were distributed around the neighborhood, and social media posts helped spread the word.

The morning of the event, Chloe felt a mix of excitement and nervousness. She wanted everything to go perfectly. As customers arrived, drawn by the heartfelt message on the posters, Chloe greeted each one with a warm smile. She explained the fundraising initiative, sharing stories about the charity and the children it helped.

Customers were moved by Chloe's
enthusiasm and dedication. They bought
cups of lemonade and generously donated
to the cause. Chloe personally thanked each
supporter, expressing her gratitude and
emphasizing the difference their
contributions would make.

The lemonade stand buzzed with energy
and compassion.

News of Chloe's effort spread quickly, drawing even more visitors. By mid-afternoon, a local reporter stopped by to interview her. "What inspired you to give back?" the reporter asked.

Chloe answered confidently, "Our community has supported my lemonade stand from the beginning. This is my way of saying thank you and helping others in need."

As the day progressed, donations poured in. Families, friends, and neighbors came together, united by a shared purpose. By the time the event ended, Chloe and her parents were overwhelmed by the outpouring of generosity. They had exceeded their fundraising goal, raising more money than they ever imagined.

That evening, as they counted the donations, Chloe's mom hugged her tightly. "Clever Chloe, you've shown how powerful kindness can be. Your dedication and compassion will make a real difference." Her dad added, "You've reminded all of us that giving back isn't just about helping others; it's about creating something bigger than ourselves."

Chloe beamed with pride. She knew this was just the beginning of her efforts to make a positive impact. Her lemonade stand had grown into more than a business—it was a symbol of community, kindness, and hope.

As the sun set, Chloe reflected on the day's success. With a full heart, she closed the stand, already dreaming of the next way she could bring people together and give back to those in need.

Reflection
and Dreams

The sun cast a warm glow on Clever Chloe's Lemonade Stand. It was a bittersweet day, as Chloe knew it marked the final chapter of her lemonade stand—at least for now. She stood behind the counter, taking in the memories and lessons she had learned along the way.

As customers approached the stand, Chloe greeted them with a mix of joy and nostalgia. She served her signature mint-infused lemonade, engaging in conversations with familiar faces. Many shared stories of how they admired her dedication and creativity.

Amidst the hustle and bustle, Chloe's parents joined her, their eyes filled with pride.

"Chloe, as we near the end of this incredible journey, let's take a moment to reflect on everything you've accomplished," her dad suggested.

Chloe nodded, her gaze drifting to the lemonade stand she had built from scratch. She reflected on the lessons she had learned: earning money, pricing, marketing, running a small business, providing exceptional customer service, and giving back to the community.

Each day brought its own challenges and rewards, shaping her into the person she was today.

Her mom placed a hand on Chloe's shoulder. "You've come a long way, Clever Chloe. You've discovered your entrepreneurial spirit and the power of perseverance. Remember, these lessons will stay with you throughout your life, guiding you toward success in whatever path you choose."

Chloe smiled, grateful for the guidance and support she had received from her parents. She realized that her journey as an entrepreneur had not only been about personal finance but had also shaped her character and instilled valuable life skills.

As the day progressed, the pace slowed down, allowing Chloe and her parents to reflect on their accomplishments and dream about the future.

"Clever Chloe, what are your dreams for the future?" her dad asked, his eyes filled with curiosity.

Chloe took a deep breath, her heart full of aspirations. "Dad, I want to continue exploring the world of entrepreneurship. I want to create new ventures, bring innovative ideas to life, and make a positive impact in the lives of others."

Her mom nodded, a twinkle in her eye. "Clever Chloe, the sky is the limit. Remember to dream big, stay true to your values, and always believe in yourself."

With a renewed sense of purpose, Chloe knew that this final chapter marked not the end, but the beginning of a lifelong journey of entrepreneurship and personal growth.

As the sun began to set on Clever Chloe's Lemonade Stand, Chloe and her parents stood together, their hands intertwined.

"Clever Chloe, we are immensely proud of you," her dad said, his voice filled with love. "You have shown us the power of a young entrepreneur's spirit, and we can't wait to see where your dreams take you."

Chloe hugged her parents tightly, gratitude swelling in her heart. "Thank you, Mom and Dad, for believing in me and supporting me every step of the way. This journey wouldn't have been possible without you."

As they closed the lemonade stand for the final time, Chloe couldn't help but feel a mix of nostalgia and excitement for the future.

With a final glance at the lemonade stand,
Chloe took her parents' hands, ready to
embark on the next chapter of her
extraordinary adventure.

What I Learned

_____

_____

_____

_____

_____

_____

_____

_____

_____

_____

_____

_____

_____

_____

_____

_____

_____

_____

_____

_____

_____

_____

ABOUT THE AUTHORS

Meet the authors of the Chloe Learns series, Rima and Greg. As parents themselves, they understand the importance of teaching children about personal finance from a young age.

Rima and Greg drew upon their own experiences growing up and the lessons they learned about money management to create Chloe's stories. They wanted to share their knowledge and insights with their own child, and ultimately with other parents and children as well.

Through Chloe's journey, Rima and Greg hope to inspire children to see money not just as something to spend, but as a tool that can help them achieve their dreams and goals. They believe that financial literacy is a critical life skill that makes a lasting impact on a child's future.

Rima and Greg are passionate about teaching children the value of saving, budgeting, and investing. They believe that these skills are key to achieving financing stability and building prosperous future. With Chloe Learns, they hope to make financial education fun, engaging, and accessible for children and parents alike.

CHLOE LEARNS

SERIES